GU00738455

NOT TO WORRY

A COMEDY

By

BARBARA VAN KAMPEN

All rights reserved. An acting fee of £ 1.50 is payable on each and every performance (50 per cent reduction for repeat performances to OAPs and Hospital Patients). Application for Performance Licence should be made to the Publishers.

Cressrelles Publishing Co Ltd

10 Station Road Industrial Estate, Colwall, Malvern
Worcestershire WR13 6RN *Telephone:* 01684 540154

WARNING

It is illegal to reproduce by any means either the whole, or any part of this play. No Amateur performances of any kind may be given (whether or NOT a charge of any kind is made) without first obtaining the written permission of the Publishers or their Agents.

Acting Fees for Performances Overseas

Apply—South Africa: Darter & Sons, Cape Town. Kenya: National Theatre, P.O. Box 452, Nairobi. Southern Rhodesia: Association of Rhodesian Theatrical Societies, P.O. Box 2701, Salisbury. Australia: Doreen Rayment, 7/62 Aubin Street, Neutral Bay 2089, N.S.W. New Zealand: Play Bureau, P.O. Box 3611, Wellington. Canada and U.S.A.: Walter H. Baker Company, Boston.

Copyright:
BARBARA VAN KAMPEN 1964

NOT TO WORRY

CAST:

Mrs. Beryl Bloom:	45 to 50. Charming, imperturbable Attractively, but comfortably dressed. Delightfully carefree.
Miss Dora Parker:	Spinster, 30 to 70. Nervously humble.
Madeleine Bloom:	Mrs. Bloom's daughter. 25, or older if Mrs. Bloom is older. Not so carefree or attractive as her mother.
Mrs. Daisy Danvers:	Charlady. Any age.
Mrs. Dodd:	Baker's wife. Any age. A woman of few words, but those few, sharp and cutting.
Mrs.Kemp:	Butcher's wife. Very aggressive. Any age.
Mrs. Payne:	Greengrocer's wife. Any age. Very timid, humble and reluctant to make trouble. Fussily dressed.

Mrs. Dodd and Mrs. Payne should contrast in height if possible, Mrs. Dodd tall and thin, Mrs. Payne, short and small.

NOT TO WORRY

A COMEDY

By

BARBARA VAN KAMPEN

SCENE:

Mrs. Bloom's sitting room. Attractively furnished. Very comfortable. Warm-coloured cushions and table lamp. A lovely vase of expensive flowers should be prominent.

BACK STAGE: *A table with a telephone. Two large ugly vases. Window L. Corner of L. and backstage a small chair, light enough to be moved forward easily.*

CENTRE STAGE: *A couch. A standard lamp behind R. of couch would look attractive. L. of couch, arm chair. R. of couch, a little in front, low tea-table. R. of couch, arm chair.*

RIGHT STAGE: *Door, well front.*

LEFT STAGE: *Door, well front. A cocktail cabinet.*

MRS. BLOOM, R. *of couch, sits absolutely content, reading the newspaper. She dips casually into a box of chocolates.*

MISS PARKER *is dusting, very ineffectively. She is wearing red rubber gloves. She comes to table back-stage and as she dusts knocks over one of a pair of vases. It smashes with a crash to the ground and breaks.*

MRS. BLOOM *takes absolutely no notice.*

Parker (*very distressed*): Oh! . . . oh! . . . (*Pause while she gazes amazed at unperturbed* BLOOM.) I've . . . I've broken something.

Bloom (*not even glancing up*): Um, um.

Parker (*anxiously*): But . . . it was a vase.

Bloom (*still reading*): Which one?

Parker (*holding up broken piece*): This one.

Bloom (*now casually looking up*): Oh, that one. I can't even remember who gave it to me. (*Snaps her finger.*) It must have been Aunt Flora.

Parker (*really distressed*): Oh! a present from your Aunt. That makes it even worse.

Bloom (*laughing*): Aunt Flora was mother's sister who ran away when she was sixteen and was never heard of again. So when we want to put the blame on someone we just go (*snaps her finger*) and say "It must have been Aunt Flora".

[*In dashes* MADELEINE L. *She wears a white overall and carries rubber boots in her hand.*]

Madeleine: What was that smash? Oh, Mother, one of the vases!

Parker (*distressed again*): I'm—I'm afraid I did it, Madeleine.

Madeleine: How could you! They are quite valuable.

Bloom (*again absorbed in her newspaper*): And quite awful . . . you're lucky. I'd probably have passed them on to you when you married.

Madeleine: But it was one of a pair.

Bloom: All the better. Now it won't matter if the other gets broken.

Parker: I feel terrible about all this . . .

Bloom: Not to worry, Dora. You go and make us all a nice cup of tea . . . and bring the chocolate walnut cake too.

Parker (*gratefully*): Oh, Beryl, you are so forgiving. I'll run and make it at once.

Madeleine (*removes white overall and hands it, with rubber boots, to* PARKER): Will you just take these too, please?

[*Exit* PARKER L.]

Madeleine: Really, Mother. Why on earth did you ask her here?

Bloom: I had no answer from my advertisement for a daily help.

Madeleine: But she's no help at all. Rubber gloves for dusting!

Bloom (*glancing up casually*): I know. But she needed a change and a holiday is impossible on her tiny income.

Madeleine (*impatiently*): And running a holiday-home for elderly spinsters is not possible on *your* tiny income.

Bloom: You might be an elderly spinster yourself one day.

Madeleine (*up-in-arms*): Thank you!

Bloom (*kindly*): Oh, don't be so serious, dear. There's that nice John Wright.

Madeleine: John! That stick-in-the-mud!

Bloom: Not so attractive as Tony Randall perhaps, but not so extravagant. Tony must look out for an heiress.

Madeleine: Indeed! . . . and talking about extravagance, I have got to warn *you*.

Bloom: Oh—er—well, another time, dear . . . I'm just reading something delightfully scandalous here. (*Settles back happily to read again.*)

Madeleine (*snatching newspaper away*): No, Mother. This time you must listen. Do you realise that the baker's, the butcher's and a dozen other bills are not paid yet?

Bloom (*unperturbed*): I'll pay them all, dear. When my next dividend comes.

Madeleine: That's not for another six weeks.

Bloom (*quite surprised*): Isn't it?

Madeleine (*angrily*): And meanwhile you go on wasting money on . . . walnut cakes and expensive flowers. They are not essential.

Bloom (*gazing happily at vase of expensive flowers*): But darling, one can't live in a house with just essentials. . . .

Madeleine (*firmly*): Mother, this is serious. When I was in the village this morning several tradesmen asked me to settle their bills.

Bloom: Not that nice Mr. Kemp the butcher, or that friendly Mr. What's-his-name, the baker. (*Laughs gaily.*) Why, Madeleine, it's just like Happy Families we used to play when you were small.

Madeleine (*sternly*): Mother, don't change the subject. The tradesmen have warned me they are coming to see you, today.

Bloom (*quickly opening cigarette box on table*): Oh, I do hope I've got enough cigarettes to go round.

Madeleine (*slowly, to give meaning*): I don't know if their *wives* smoke.

Bloom (*puzzled*): Their wives?

Madeleine: Your ·ruse of playing the "helpless-little-widow" to the tradesmen is up. This time their wives are coming.

Bloom (*a little concerned*): Oh . . . yes . . . that's different.

Madeleine: Very different.

Bloom (*contemplating*): Now, what will be the best approach? "Let us talk this over woman-to-woman", or "Of course men do not understand, but housewives like ourselves . . ." That's rather good, isn't it? Sort of "letting-our-hair-down-together".

Madeleine: It won't work, Mother. They want their accounts settled.

Bloom: But if I haven't got it I haven't got it. (*Cheerfully*) Oh, not to worry, Madeleine. Something is sure to turn up.

Madeleine: The only thing certain to turn up is a group of angry tradesmen's wives.

Bloom: Darling, you *are* pessimistic. Why, remember that time when I hadn't a penny, and I suddenly found two ten pound notes that I'd used as a bookmark?

Madeleine: That was just a stroke of luck.

Bloom: Oh, I wouldn't say that, dear. Remember that lump of stone we used to prop open the garage door with until someone offered us a thousand pounds for it and we discovered it was an early Henry Moore?

Madeleine: But there are no Henry Moores or ten pound notes this time.

Bloom: No. Pity, isn't it? Never mind dear, not to worry. You're so nervy lately. I expect it's all this worrying about if you will see Tony Randall again.

Madeleine: As a matter of fact, he may be taking me to the County Club this evening.

Bloom (*not very hopeful*): Oh yes? (*Shrugs her shoulders.*) Oh well, darling, *if* he does ring, you run off and enjoy yourself. (*Eagerly*) I know! You go and have a marvellous hair-do like this (*indicates picture in newspaper.*) Go to Antonio and put it on my account.

Madeleine: And have Mrs. Antonio joining the baker and the butcher's wives marching up the drive! *No* thank thank you.

Bloom (*settling back comfortably again*): My dear Madeleine, you are making a mountain out of a mole-hill. Why, these bills . . .

Madeleine: You'll see. . . . (*Bell rings.* MADELEINE *triumphantly*) What did I say!

[*Enter* PARKER L. *carrying tea things and a cake on a tray.*]

Parker: Just a moment, just a moment. I'm coming.

Madeleine (*taking tea things from her*). First see who it is from the window.

> [PARKER *hurries to window and by pressing nose to window and looking as far* L. *as possible, she can see the front door.*]

Madeleine: Male or female?

Parker: Oh definitely female.

Madeleine (*triumphantly nodding at her mother*): What did I tell you!

Parker: Shall I show her in here?

Bloom (*unperturbed*): Why of course. How lucky we can offer her tea.

> [*Exit* PARKER *hurriedly* L.]

Madeleine (*grimly*): She'll want your "pound of flesh", not tea!

Bloom (*airily*): Oh, I didn't know we were expecting a cannibal!

> [PARKER *appears in doorway* L.]

Parker: Here is—er——

> [DANVERS *enters* L., *pushing past* PARKER. *She comes sailing cheerfully in. Her hat is adorned with a prominent feather.*

Danvers: Mrs. Danvers, Daisy Danvers, is the name.

Bloom (*all charm, rises and offers her hand to* DANVERS): How nice of you to call, Mrs. Danvers. Do sit down.

Danvers (*hesitates just a moment*): Er—Thanks, I will. (*Sits in chair* R.)

> [BLOOM *sits* R. *of couch again.*]

Madeleine (*anxious to get* PARKER *out of the room*): Oh—er—Miss Parker. I expect you would enjoy a few moments to yourself. (*Very hastily pours out cup of tea and thrusts it into* PARKER'S *hand.*) Why not take this up to your room.

Parker (*a little dazed. Disappointed too*): Well—er—yes, if you say so. I do enjoy a cup of tea. (*Pointedly eyes cake*) and—er—a little something with it.

Danvers (*friendly, heartily*): Just what my old Mum used to say. You can forget the tea as long as you don't forget the drop of rum in it.

Parker (*horrified*): Oh, but really, that wasn't my meaning. I never touch . . .

Madeleine (*very hurriedly cuts piece of cake, puts it on a plate and thrusts it into* PARKER'S *hands.*): Here you are. (*Almost pushes dazed* PARKER *to door.*) And no need to hurry down again.

[*Exit* PARKER. MADELINE *turns back into room, giving slight sigh of relief.*]

Bloom: Would you care for a cup of tea, Mrs. Danvers?

Danvers (*sitting back and spreading herself out comfortably*): Well, I don't mind if I do.

Bloom (*pouring tea and handing cup to* DANVERS): And a little piece of cake?

Danvers: Won't say no to that neither. (MADELEINE *reluctantly starts to cut cake.*) And not so much of the "little piece" either, ducks. (MADELEINE *reluctantly cuts slightly larger piece and hands it on a plate to* DANVERS, *then sits* L.)

Bloom (*all charm*): This is an unexpected visit, Mrs. Danvers. (*Endeavouring to make pleasant conversation.*) How is your good man. Business good?

Danvers: Can't say, dearie. Him being the attendant at the "Gents' " in the market square.

[*Bewildered look on faces of* MADELEINE *and* BLOOM.]

Bloom (*puzzled, to* MADELEINE): But . . . but even *I* can't have run up a bill there, can I, Madeleine? There must be some mistake. (*To* DANVERS) Why exactly are you here?

Danvers: Your advertisement, dearie.

Madeleine (*quickly removing cake out of Danvers' reach*): For a charwoman.

Danvers (*on her dignity*): For a housewife's lady-assistant.

Bloom (*very charming at once*): Of course. How silly of me. You see I was expecting other callers . . .

Danvers: First of all then, ducks, me terms. I starts at ten o'clock and leaves at three.

Bloom: Yes . . .

Danvers: And I likes me elevenses at half-past ten.

Bloom: Yes.

Danvers: An hour-and-a-half for me lunch.

Bloom: It seems a little on the long side . . .

Danvers: And one of them little radios for me apron pocket as I works.

Bloom: Yes, I see. And how much an hour are you asking?

Danvers: Ten bob an hour . . . insurance extra, of course.

Bloom (*very pleased and agreeable*): Of course.

[*Very loud warning cough from* MADELEINE. BLOOM, *subdued, alters her tone.*]

Oh, I forgot. No, I'm afraid I couldn't pay all that.

Danvers (*on her dignity*): All we ladies ask that now, dear.

Bloom: Couldn't you make it a little less?

Danvers: All depends. What are the perks? I means, any little "unexpected extras" that come my way?

Bloom (*candidly*): I'm afraid none. (*Sympathetically.*) I'm always hoping that myself too.

Danvers: Then I'm afraid you won't suit me, dearie. We ladies only obliges——

[*Front door bell rings.* MADELEINE, *alarmed, quickly crosses to window, looks out, turns and nods her head at* BLOOM.]

Madeleine: It's a little blue car.

> [MADELEINE, *very hurried exit* L.]

Danvers: Well then, I'll be off. (BLOOM *very relieved until she sees* DANVERS *settle back comfortably in her chair, plate with cake on her knee.*) I'll just finish me cake first. (*Beams all over her face.*) Waste not, want not, eh, dearie.

> [*Enter* KEMP L. *angrily waving umbrella, followed by anxious* MADELEINE L.]

Kemp: So *there* you are, Mrs. Bloom. Your daughter tried to stop me coming in.

Bloom: Inded? But who exactly are you?

Kemp (*very militant*): Who am I!! I'm Mrs. Kemp, the butcher's wife. You owe my old man five weeks.

Bloom (*quiet aside to* MADELEINE): Ah, your lady for a pound of flesh. (*To* KEMP) Five weeks? Are you sure?

Kemp (*addressing everyone in general*): Yes I am. (*Pulls bill out of her pocket and reads.*) Listen to this. Sweetbreads, two calves' tongues, six kidneys.

Bloom (*graciously*): Ah yes, the kidneys were delicious.

Kemp: So I should think! There's nothing wrong with my old man's kidneys!

Madeleine (*anxious to get rid of* DANVERS *as soon as possible*): Just a moment, Mrs. Kemp. I think Mrs. Danvers wishes to be going.

Danvers (*having followed the conversation with great interest*): Going? Not me, ducks. This is just getting interesting. (*Settles back even more comfortably, beaming all over her face.*)

Kemp (*to* BLOOM): I warn you I want this settled or no more meat delivered here.

Bloom (*confidently assured*): But of course. I'll write you a cheque at once.

Kemp: *No* cheques, thank you. I want cash, straight away, before the other tradesmen's wives get here.

[*Front door bell rings.* BLOOM *bites her lip, slightly anxious.* MADELINE *very agitated.*]

Madeleine: I'll go, Mother. (*Brightly false*) I expect it's it's the postman.

[*Exit* MADELEINE.]

Kemp: Well I don't! I'm not the only one coming, you know.

Bloom (*gushingly*): Oh. How nice. It will be quite a party.

Danvers: A guilty party you mean, ducks!

[*Enter* MADELEINE L., *showing anxiety.*]

Madeleine: Here are two visitors to see you, Mother.

[*Enter* DODD. *She is extremely plainly dressed. He arms crossed on her chest, shoulders high, her chi, well drawn in. She surveys* BLOOM *over her steel rimmed glasses.*]

Madeleine: This is Mrs. Dodd. The baker's wife.

Danvers (*chuckling*): Come for her dough!

Dodd (*sharply*): Good afternoon.

[*Enter* PAYNE L., *all of a flutter with embarrassment, which makes her a litle giggly.*]

Madeleine: And this is Mrs. Payne, the greengrocers's wife.

Danvers (*chuckling aside to* MADELEINE): A pain-in-the-neck she means, eh ducks?

Payne: Pleased to meet you, I'm sure . . . I hardly like coming like this . . but well . . . you know how it is——

Dodd (*sharply*): She means you owe us both money, *and* we mean to have it.

Bloom (*still unperturbed*): Oh really? But won't you sit down?

Payne: Thank you . . . most kind I'm sure. (*Sits in chair* L.)

Dodd: I prefer to stand.

Bloom: A cup of tea, Mrs. Payne.

Payne: Oh yes . . . Nothing like the cup that cheers, is there?

Dodd: Time for cheering when this is paid. (*Flings out her hand holding bill.*)

Bloom: Oh, but first a cup of tea . . .

Dodd: *No thank you.*

Bloom: A piece of cake then?

Dodd: My cake you mean.

Bloom (*a little subdued and taken aback*): Oh yes. It's not paid for yet, is it?

Payne (*Very reluctant to have to say this*): One or two other things, too, I'm afraid. (*A little awkwardly takes bill from her handbag and reads.*) Including half-a-dozen peaches, five pounds hothouse grapes, a dozen artichokes . . . (*Timidly*) Rather expensive items, aren't they? When you haven't even paid for the potatoes yet.

Dodd (*sharply*): Nor for (*opens handbag, takes out bill, and violently snaps handbag shut*) a dozen cream buns, six rum babas, a walnut cake, a chocolate cake, three dozen éclairs——

Danvers: 'Ave a heart, ducks. You're making my mouth water!

Dodd (*slamming her bill down violently on the table*): Here you are. Nine pounds fifteen shillings and four pence.

Kemp (*slamming her bill down too*): And this. Twelve pounds, five and eightpence.

Payne (*timidly, hardly daring to put her bill on table*): Well—er—fifteen pounds, eleven shillings and eightpence ha'penny.

Bloom (*trying to be humorous*): Well, I might manage the ha'penny, Mrs. Payne. (*She laughs falsely merrily, hoping the others will too. They do not.* BLOOM'S *face falls.*)

Kemp (*staring, fixedly angry, at* BLOOM): We want to know what you are going to do about this.

Payne: That's what *I* want to know. (*Also looks fixedly at* BLOOM.)

Dodd: And what I want to know. (*Also looks fixedly at* BLOOM.)

Madeleine (*swallowing lump in her throat, raising eyes to heaven and murmuring to herself*): And what I want to know too. (*Also looks anxiously, fixedly at* BLOOM.)

[*Pause as all look fixedly at* BLOOM. *She looks seriously from one to the other, biting her lip. She then leans forward, gazing itno space. Suddenly her face lights up for a flickering moment. She has an idea. She turns to* MADELEINE *and snaps her fingers. Then she quickly adopts an expression of sad, deep suffering.*

Bloom (*quietly*): Please, ladies, may I ask you to lower your voices a little. Madeleine, did I hear Aunt Flora call? (*Glances up at the ceiling. The others look up too, then back again, very puzzled but intrigued, at* BLOOM.) No. I think I am mistaken. But you know how it is when there is a sick relative in the house.

Dodd (*very interested*): Oh, something serious?

Bloom (*with tragic expression*): Hopeless, I'm afraid.

Payne: Oh terrible . . . the poor soul.

Bloom: It's my dear Aunt Flora. Over ninety. No hope of recovery, of course.

Danvers (*very sympathetic*): Oh, sorry, ducks.

Bloom: Yes. (*Sighs.*) Very sad. But I do all I can to make her last hours happy. I'm her only relative in the world.

Danvers (*eagerly*): Oh, and got a nice bit of . . . you know (*rubs first finger and thumb together to indicate money*).

Bloom (*sadly*): Rolling in it . . . (*Dramatically*) Oh, the sadness of it. There she lies, a woman of great wealth. yet no longer able to enjoy the simplest of pleasures.

Payne (*dabbing at her eyes with handkerchief*): You are beginning to make me cry!

Kemp: Me too.

Bloom (*sadly dabbing at her eyes with handkerchief*): I'm beginning to make myself cry too!

Dodd (*gruffly, but subdued by sad story*): We knew nothing about this of course.

Bloom: Now you can understand why I ordered so generously but (*gulps back a sob*) I was trying to bring a little pleasure into dear Aunt Flora's closing hours.

Danvers (*shocked*): You make her sound like a pub!

Kemp (*nodding her head thoughtfully*): Ah, now I understand. The sweetbreads——

Payne (*nodding head*): The peaches——

Dodd (*nodding head*): The éclairs——

Bloom (*also nodding head*): All for dear Auntie. (*Starts.*) Ah! I heard her then. Madeleine, call Sister Dora, will you? (MADELEINE *looks blank and puzzled.*) Madeleine, are you dreaming? I said "Call *Sister Dora*".

Madeleine (*still dazed*): Yes—yes Mother. I'll call her at once.

[*Exit* MADELEINE L.]

Bloom: But to return to your visits, I shall of course settle your little accounts. Aunt Flora must not be deprived of her last few pleasures, her grapes, her sweetbreads. . . .

Dodd: Of course not, but——

Bloom (*nonchalantly*): Not to worry, Mrs. Dodd. Aunt Flora has an account at Fortnum & Mason's. I bought locally because—well, it seemed only fair to patronize one's local tradesmen, but as things are . . .

[*Enter* PARKER L. *She has Madeleine's white overall on and a white cloth folded on her head as a nurse's headdress.*]

Bloom: Oh, Nurse Dora, there you are. (*Anxious to get her out of the room before she gives the game away.*) Hurry up, please nurse. I heard her crying.

Parker (*absolutely bewildered*): Yes—yes of course. It's time for her bottle. . . .

Payne (*sentimentally*): Oh how nice. She's had a baby!

Kemp: At over ninety? Don't be ridiculous!

Parker (*holding up hot water bottle*): I mean this . . . if you'll excuse me. (*Scurried exit* R.)

Dodd: We didn't realise things were so serious.

Bloom (*furtively fingers bills on table. Is alarmed at figures so is forgetful for a moment*): Neither did I. (*Quickly recalls her pose. Very sadly*) I mean, neither did I until tonight.

Payne (*sniffling*): The poor dear.

[*Enter* MADELEINE L. *She stands anxiously listening to conversation.*]

Bloom (*sadly*): I'm afraid I let my heart run away with my head. All these bills——

Danvers (*cheerily*): What have you got to worry about. The old girl's rolling in it, and you're her only relation in the world! Why, Bob's-your-uncle!

Bloom (*forgetting herself, chuckles*): Flora's my aunt, you mean.

Madeleine (*hurriedly*): Mother.

Bloom (*recovering herself quickly, adopts doleful tone again*): Ah, when that sad day arrives I shall be richer in worldly goods but poorer in the loss of a dearly beloved aunt.

Payne (*Sniffing*): So sad. (*Wipes her nose delicately.*)

Kemp (*sniffing loudly*): So sad. (*Blows her nose violently.*)

Dodd (*sniffing sharply*): So Sad. (*Blows her nose firmly.*)

> [*Enter* PARKER R., *begins to scuttle hurriedly across to* L. *She carries tea-cup on tray.*]

Payne (*sympathetically*): Ah nurse, how is the poor old dear now?

> [PARKER *absolutely at loss what to say, gazes anxiously at* BLOOM, *then at* MADELEINE.]

Bloom (*anxious to get* PARKER *away*): Just about the same, eh, nurse?

Parker (*bewildered*): Er—yes—just about the same——

Bloom (*brightly*): Well, we must not keep you from your duty, must we, nurse?

> [PARKER, *confused, moves towards* L.]

Madeleine (*anxious to get her away, grabs her arm and steers her quickly to the door* L.): If there's anything you need, just call me.

Parker (*still stands open-mouthed in the doorway*): Er—I don't understand——

Madeleine (*with a push sends her out through doorway*): I said "Just call me".

> [PARKER *hurried exit* L. MADELEINE *shuts door after her and sighs with relief.*]

Danvers: A bit slow in the up-take, ain't she?

Bloom: Ah! but highly qualified, and so quiet and restful in everything she does.

> [*Loud crash of falling tea cup and saucer off stage* L. *All jump with surprise.*]

Danvers: Sez you! But give me our district nurse every time!

Dodd (*beginning to get ready to leave*): What you have told us has certainly made a difference to our visit.

Bloom: Yes, I hoped it would . . . I mean, I thought it would.

Kemp: Seeing as how things are going to change for the better so soon.

Kemp (*sitting suddenly upright*): I've just remembered (*Looks cunningly from* DODD *to* PAYNE *and screwing her mouth in a firm line.*) There's something fishy going on here.

Payne (*nervously*): Er—here?

Bloom: You must be mistaken. The fishmonger's wife hasn't arrived—yet.

Kemp (*looking severely at* BLOOM): Dr. Henderson was in the shop only this morning.

Danvers (*all interest, leans eagerly forward*): Yes, go on, ducks——

Kemp: I just casually asked him if he was busy and he said——

Payne (*anxiously*): Yes?——

Kemp (*triumphantly*): He said fortunately there wasn't a serious illness in the whole neighbourhood at the moment.

[BLOOM *a little taken aback.* MADELEINE *looks very anxious.*]

Payne (*tremulously pointing to ceiling*): You mean, what about her, up there?

Kemp: Yes, her up there.

Danvers (*indignantly to* BLOOM): 'Ere, you said she was breathing her last.

Dodd (*sharply, with emphasis*): Yes, Mrs. Bloom. Can you explain that?

[*A very tense pause as all look at* BLOOM. *For a moment she is taken aback, then turns a charming but sad smile on them.*]

Bloom: But of course I can. Dr. Henderson is a dear. I myself could not ask for a better doctor. But—(*she shrugs her shoulders*) you know how it is when money is no object.

Danvers: Well, can't say I've had any experience myself!

Bloom: You're not the only one. (*Quickly adopts a less frivolous tone.*) No, no, of course, but dear Aunt Flora can always satisfy her slightest whim, so when she demanded a Harley Street specialist, well . . . hopeless as it is, how could I deny her her dying wish?

[*All are sympathetic again.*]

Dodd: That's so.

Danvers: Just what I always says myself. "A little of what you fancy does you good.

Kemp (*suddenly alert again*): Just a minute. I haven't heard of any doctor coming here.

Dodd (*again alert*): You're right. And you know how it is in our village. Nobody misses anything.

[*All again stare questioningly at* Bloom. Bloom *gazes back at each in turn, then smiles as if producing her trump card.*]

Bloom: Nobody has seen him.

Kemp (*Smiling contemptuously*): So I begin to think!

Bloom (*graciously unperturbed*): The specialist is staying here in the house.

[Madeleine *visibly agitated and bewildered.*]

Dodd: Here?

Payne: In this house?

Danvers: Seeing's believing, ducks——

Bloom: But of course. Madeleine. I know the specialist is waiting to see Aunt Flora. Will you please tell Dr. Parker he can go up to Auntie now?

Madeleine (*aghast*): Dr.—Dr. Parker?

Bloom: Yes, deaf. Just go and see if you can assist him. Help him fasten up the back of his operating gown or anything like that.

Madeleine: Yes—of course—if you say so, Mother.

[*Exit* Madeleine L., *very puzzled.*]

Payne (*a little faintly*): Did I hear you say *operating* gown? Oh—er—— (*She faints, slips forward in her chair.*)

[*All lean forward anxiously.* DODD *bends over her.*]

Dodd (*anxiously*): What is it?

Payne (*coming to, speaks faintly*): Nothing, nothing really. Silly me. I always come over faint at the very mention of blood——

Bloom: Now, now, Mrs. Payne, not to worry. I appreciate your sympathy, but (*ruefully*) this is a sorrow I must carry alone. Ah! I believe I hear the specialist coming now. (*All heads turn to door* L.) I am afraid I must ask you not to address him or attract his attention in any way. You know how surgeons are before big operations—concentration, concentration, nothing but concentration . . . ah! here he is. (*Finger to mouth.*) Shush! ——

[*All lean forward in awe as door opens* L. MADELEINE *enters* L. *then stands back for* PARKER *to enter. Enter* PARKER L. *She has white overall put on back to front, rubber gloves again, and* MADELEINE'S *rubber boots on. She has a white cap on her head and a white cloth over her mouth and nose. Only her eyes are visible, and over these she has a large pair of spectacles. In her hand she carries a bread knife. She walks very deliberately across from* L. *to* R., *her eyes fixed on nothing but the door* R. *All gaze at her in awesome fascination.*]

Bloom (*in impressive whisper*): This is the world-famous surgeon, Doctor Parker.

Danvers (*jokes, but is visibly awed and speaks in a whisper*): Can't exactly call him a Nosey-Parker, can you?

Bloom (*whispering*): Ah. Dedicated to his work, quite, quite dedicated.

Danvers (*head thrust forward, gazes with awe and curiosity at* PARKER): But—but he's got a bread knife in his hand! He ain't going to operate with *that*, is he?

Bloom (*trying casually to laugh it off: gives a gay little laugh*): Ah, you know what they say. It's a poor workman who finds fault with his tools.

[*Exit* PARKER.]

Kemp (*no longer whispering*): May be, but if I had to choose between my old man or him doing any cuttin'-up, give me my old man every time.

[PAYNE *gives a moan and falls back faint in her chair.*]

Danvers: Whoops, dearie, she's off again.

Madeleine (*gives a little shriek*): Oh!

Bloom: Why, so she is!

Danvers: Fainted right off, she has.

[*All gather round* PAYNE.]

Dodd (*leaning over* PAYNE): We must bring her round at once. (*Brightly*) Smacking the face helps, I've heard. (*Gives* PAYNE *a resounding smack on the face. The sound of the smack to be made very loudly off stage. No effect on* PAYNE, *who remains limp.*]

Kemp: I know, burn a feather under her nose.

Bloom (*looking round anxiously*): But where can we find a feather? (*Her eyes light up as she sees feather in* DANVERS' *hat.*)

Danvers (*claps hand to her hat*): Oh no you don't, ducks. You try giving her a drop of gin first.

Bloom (*dashing to cocktail cabinet*): A good idea! (*Takes out bottle of gin.*)

Kemp: I think brandy is better.

Bloom (*taking out bottle of brandy*): Brandy then.

[BLOOM *pours out glass of brandy.*]

Danvers (*a little huffed*): Well, I swears by gin.

Bloom (*cheerfully*): No time for arguments. You give her brandy (*hands glass of brandy to* KEMP *and pours glass of gin and hands it to* DANVERS) and you gin.

[KEMP *pours drink down* PAYNE'S *throat. All lean forward and anxiously gaze at* PAYNE, *who shows no sign of life.*]

Danvers (*triumphantly*): What did I say, dearie? Now let me try. (*Pours drink down* PAYNE'S *throat. Again all lean forward anxiously. Again* PAYNE *shows no sign of life.*)

Bloom: Not a flicker.

Madeleine (*panicking*): What can we do now?

Bloom: I've got it. Those pep pills I bought.

Kemp: Pep pills!

Danvers (*a little anxious*): Sure they're safe, dearie?

Bloom (*airily*): Perfectly. All they did to me was make me talk such a lot. (*Laughs.*) Do you remember, MADELEINE? I went on and on.

Danvers (*looking at lifeless* PAYNE): Well she's not exactly chatty at the moment, is she? Might be just the thing for her.

Bloom: Now where did I put them (*opens handbag*). Oh yes, there're one or two loose in the bottom of my bag. (*Takes one out.*) One enough, do you think? No, better make it two and be on the safe side. (*Takes out another and looks round.*) Any water anywhere? Oh well, not to worry. Brandy will do just as well. (*Pours out another glass of brandy.*)

[*All gather round* PAYNE, *anxious but excited.*]

Kemp: I'll hold her head.

Dodd: I'll hold her hands.

Danvers (*bending over in awkward attitude, with hands on* PAYNE'S *ankles*): And I'll take her feet. (*Gazes up at* PAYNE.) Lor, it's like that Cape Kennedy and waiting for the count-down. All together now. Ten, nine——

[*All solemnly join in.*]

All: Eight—seven—six—five—four—three—two—one . . .

Danvers: And in they go.

[BLOOM *forces pills into* PAYNE'S *mouth, then makes her drink.*]

Bloom: Now——

[*All anxiously watch* PAYNE. *There is a moment's dead silence, nobody moves.*]

Danvers: Awful quiet, ain't it?

[*A second's pause.* PAYNE *suddenly sits bolt upright. Keenly alive, she talks non-stop. No longer shy and timid, she is positively brazen.*]

Payne: Hullo, girls! What are you all looking so glum about? Ho, ho, I remember. (*Points her finger up to ceiling.*) Poor old Auntie upstairs. Well, it's an ill wind blows no-one any good, eh, Mrs. Bloom. That's what I always say. You never can tell——

Bloom (*a little alarmed, trying to get a word in*): But Mrs. Payne, I——

Payne (*talking at a great speed, non-stop*): Just you look on the bright side, my dear. Why I remember many a time when if I hadn't looked on the bright side things might have turned out very different, very different indeed——

Danvers (*alarmed*): Sure you're feeling all right, ducks?

Payne (*gaily*): Perfectly well, just perfect. You'll see, Mrs. Bloom, you just mark my words.

[*All looking exhausted at her non-stop talk.*]

Don't you worry and worry won't worry you. Everything will be all right, do you hear me? (*With expansive gesture*) Perfectly all right.

Bloom (*gazes horrified at Payne*): Heavens, it's the pep pills!

Madeleine (*horrified*): With the brandy and gin!

Kemp (*firmly*): I think we'd better get her home.

Payne (*loudly, gaily*): Splendid idea. (*Springs to her feet.*) Then I can spread the good tidings around the village. I'll tell them money will be pouring in here in a matter of days. (*Leans forward very friendly and eager.*) I'll let my friend Mrs. Smith, the fishmonger's wife, know at once. So if you fancy a dover sole——

Madeleine (*quickly cutting in*): Sole is a little too dear——

Payne: Come now (*coaxingly, and digging* MADELEINE *in the ribs.*) Sole isn't dear for the dear old soul upstairs, eh? (*Jerks her finger up towards the ceiling and chuckles.*)

Bloom: It's very kind of you, but——

Payne: No but about it. And what about a nice lobster for yourself?

Bloom (*pleased, settles back contentedly on couch again*): Well, I do rather enjoy a lobster.

Payne (*expansively*): And why not? I'll tell her. (*Arms flung wide.*) I'll tell everyone——

Kemp (*to* DODD): We'd better get her home, quickly. (*They take* PAYNE *by the arm.*)

Madeleine (*cuttingly*): I couldn't agree more.

Payne (*not at all abashed and talking non-stop*): Good idea, girls. Home we go. (*Bright idea comes to her.*) I'll drive.

Kemp: Oh no you don't——

Payne: Just as you like. (*Catching sight of glasses and bottles on table, lurches towards them.*) But what about one for the road first, eh?

Dodd: Most certainly not. Come along now, Mrs. Payne.

[DODD *and* KEMP *try pulling* PAYNNE *to door* L.]

Payne: All in good time, I always say——

Dodd: Yes, yes, I know you do, but come along.

[PAYNE *still will not budge.*]

Payne (*still rattling amiably on*): As for our little accounts. Forget them, eh girls?

Kemp (*in despair to* DANVERS): Lend us a hand, will you please?

Danvers: Right you are, ducks. (*Pushes from behind.*) Now, all together——

Bloom: Thank you, Mrs. Danvers.

[*They have nearly pushed* PAYNE *to door.*]

Danvers: Thanks granted, dearie.

Payne (*gaily*): Thanks granted too, dear.

[*They have now got* PAYNE *to door.*]

Danvers (*suddenly calls back over her shoulder to* BLOOM): · There, I forgot. Is Auntie about my size? You know, coats and things like that?

Bloom (*puzzled*): Your size? (*Idea dawns.*) Oh yes, just your size and masses and masses of clothes. I don't know how I shall ever get rid of them.

Danvers: *I* do, ducks. (*Winks.*) And under those circumstances I'll make it half-a-crown an hour. So don't forget, dearie.

Payne (*gaily*): No, don't forget, Mrs. Bloom. Just let us know anything you want.

Kemp (*calls back while still struggling to get* PAYNE *through doorway*): A nice piece of steak——

Dodd (*also calling back*): Or one of our new Viennese Flans——

Payne (*very expansive and happy*): That's right. Ring up for the lot. (*Begins to sing "When it rains it only rains pennies from heaven".*)

[*Exit* L. PAYNE, *with a sudden jerk as she is pulled by* DODD *and* KEMP *and pushed by* DANVERS. *Exit* DANVERS, KEMP *and* DODD L. *Strains of* PAYNE *still singing are heard as she departs, off stage.*]

Bloom (*calmly sitting back again and picking up newspaper*): So that's the bills settled until my next dividend comes. Is there any tea left?

Madeleine (*sharply*): Mother, how could you lead them on like that!

Bloom (*airily*): Quite easily, my dear, and no harm done. (*chuckles.*) In fact it seems to have done Mrs. Payne a world of good.

[*Enter* PARKER R. *She is unconsciously holding bread knife in a menacing position and she is still dressed as a surgeon. Bloom, catching sight of her, gives a little shriek.*]

Parker (*peering right and left over her mask*): Have they gone?

Bloom (*relaxed again*): You had me scared for a moment.

Parker: Not so scared as I was when that poor soul fainted. I was afraid they'd call on me as a doctor.

Madeleine (*horrified*): Oh! I didn't think of that.

Parker (*near tears, her voice quivering*): Well *I* did. I know I agreed to come and assist you in any way but I didn't think it would include nursing and surgery.

Bloom (*turning on her most charming manner*): But Dora, you did it all so beautifully. Now didn't she, Madeleine? You were most convincing.

Parker (*looking rather pleased and flattered but hardly daring to believe it*): Was I really?

Bloom: You must have been. Look how poor Mrs. Payne passed out at the very sight of you.

Parker (*very pleased with herself*): Yes, she did, didn't she? And it was all my own idea to put on the overall back to front!

Bloom: My dear Dora, you were perfectly awe-inspiring. If Mr. Alfred Hitchcock had seen you he'd have snapped you up at once for one of his horror films.

Madeleine: But now I think you had better lie down and rest for a while.

Parker: Perhaps I will. (*Crosses over to door* L., *still very pleased with herself.*) But don't forget me if you need any help again. I'll take on any role you like, from Florence Nightingale (*laughing and quite amazed at her own daring*) to Cleopatra!

[*Exit* PARKER L. *Telephone rings.* MADELEINE *dashes eagerly to answer it.*]

Madeleine (*at phone*): Maypark, eight-eight-six-three. Madeleine Bloom speaking. . . . (*Disappointment show in her face and voice.*) Oh yes. I'll call her. (*Listlessly*) For you, Mother. It's the fishmonger.

Bloom: Oh! (*Drawing a long face at* MADELEINE *and takes 'phone. She uses her "charming" voice*) Ah, good afternoon, Mr. Smith. About my account. I hope . . . (*Very pleased*) Oh! *not* about my account . . . trout? Just come in, you say . . . but how nice of you to think of us first. . . . Yes, I would like some. (*Aside to* MADELEINE) You like trout, don't you dear? (*Into 'phone*) Yes, send them up, Mr. Smith, but (*a little cautiously*) Er—about adding them to my account . . . (*Again pleasantly surprised.*) No need to worry. (*Smiles.*) Oh, then I certainly won't. Thank you, Mr. Smith. Goodbye. (*Sits down, happily at ease.*) Thank heavens for pep pills.

Madeleine: What do you mean?

Bloom: Mrs. Payne is evidently spreading the good news of our future fortune all round the village.

Madeleine: And when they find out the truth?

Bloom (*chuckling*): Oh, dear Aunt Flora can linger quite a while yet.

Madeleine (*resigned*): Well, I'm going back to my gardening. (*Anxiously*) You'll call me if Tony phones, won't you?

Bloom (*tenderly serious*): Madeleine dear, you know he won't ring you. Oh, he's charming enough but he has got far too extravagant ideas.

Madeleine (*sarcastically*): Then I should have thought you and he had a lot in common!

Bloom (*pretending to be hurt, but really amused*): Oh! I shall certainly have to put down a saucer of milk for you, my dear.

Madeleine (*has to laugh, even against her will*): Mother, you are incorrigible.

Bloom (*laughs*): : I'm glad you realise it.

[*Exit* MADELEINE L. BLOOM *sits back again, humming "Pennies from Heaven".*]

Bloom (*laughs to herself*): That ought to be my signature tune.

[*Telephone rings.* BLOOM *answers it.*]

Bloom (*on 'phone*): Maypark, eight-eight-six-three. Mrs. Bloom speaking. (*Look of surprise. She quickly peers out of window to see where* MADELEINE *is.*) Oh, it's you, Tony . . . Madeleine? . . . Oh, I'm afraid she's not here at the moment . . . (*Surprised tone*) You want to take her to the Country Club? This is rather sudden, isn't it? (*Idea suddenly dawns on her.*) Oh! and where are you phoning from . . . the village Post Office. I thought so . . . and you've heard our news I expect . . . hum—hum—— (*Laughs gaily.*) Yes, she *does* talk a lot doesn't she? It was the pep pills I gave her. (*Chuckles.*) Yes, I did, really. That's why she's talking such nonsense—— (*Conspiratorially*) Not a word, Tony, but I haven't even got an Aunt Flora here, but it postpones paying my bills until my allowance is due . . . (*Laughs.*) Yes, it *was* rather clever, wasn't it? (*Laughs merrily, amused at what Tony has just said on 'phone.*) My dear Tony, even *if* I were twenty years younger *I* wouldn't marry *you*!!! . . . oh! so you believe in birds of a feather flock together . . . (*Glances out of window and sees* MADELEINE *approaching. She changes her voice completely and pretends to be talking to the greengrocer's wife.*) No, I don't care for figs, Mrs. Payne . . . (*Enter* MADELEINE L.) But thank you for offering them to me. Goodbye . . . goodbye. (*Hangs up receiver.*) Those pep pills have turned Mrs. Payne into a positive Harvest Festival. (*Pleased as idea comes to her.*) I've got an idea! While the tide has, so to speak, turned in my favour, we might ask a few friends to dinner. Why don't you ask that nice John Wright.

Madeleine (*coldly*): I'd rather ask Tony.

Bloom (*forgetting herself*): So would I—— (*Hurriedly*) I mean, you must be sensible, dear. If I had a fortune and could give you an allowance of your own there is nobody I'd like better than Tony for a son-in-law but (*she shrugs her shoulders ruefully*) beggars can't be choosers, Madeleine. (*Sits down and again picks up newspaper.*)

Madeleine (*sighs*): I suppose not. Like poor Miss Parker having to act all those parts.

Bloom (*reading newspaper as she speaks*): Oh, I think she's very pleased with herself now. (*Sits bolt upright and gives a little shriek as she reads something in the newspaper.*)

Madeleine (*runs to her*): What is it, Mother?

Bloom (*aghast*): Madeleine, just look at this . . . (*points to a column in the newspaper.*)

Madeleine (*reading from paper*): "Wealthy recluse dies. A large fortune has been left by an aged recluse, Miss Flora Farrington, who died alone in her mansion near Paris. So far no living relative can be traced."

Bloom (*delighted*): Paris! Oh I adore Paris. (*Delighted as sudden idea comes to her.*) My dear, you and Tony can use the mansion for your honeymoon!

Madeleine (*dazed, asks quickly*): What do you mean? But—but—who is it?

Bloom (*snaps her fingers and laughs*): It's Aunt Flora. The one who left home and was never heard of again. I'm her nearest relation! (*She leans back contentedly in her chair and smiles happily at the notice in the paper.*) What am I always telling you, Madeleine? Not to worry!

CURTAIN